Vine Doodle

A Coloring Book

BY

Felipe Rocha

This book is dedicated
to

Peanut, Olive and Noah

Acknowledgements

1.............................Lauren Oram's post on Vine

2.............................Porscha Coleman's post on Vine

3.............................Dominic Licciardi's Post on Vine

4.............................Katie Ryan's post on Vine

5.............................Jeffery Walter's post on Vine

6.............................Deborah G. Bryant (MommaDee) Love & Hip Hop: Atlanta

7.............................FNAFboy's post on Vine

8.............................Jimmy Ustar's post on Vine

9.............................Adam Perkin's post on Vine

10.............................Christine Sydelko's post on Vine

11.............................Lenarr's post on Vine

12.............................terryjr12's post on Vine

13.............................Andrew Proctor's post on Vine

14.............................THECECESHOW's post on Vine

15.............................Nick Mastodon's post on Vine

16.............................Marisa Belsky's post on Vine

17.............................Father Time's post on Vine

18.............................JimmyHere's post on Vine

Acknowledgements

19................................Rachel Olson's post on Vine

20................................Josh Kennedy's post on Vine

21................................Kong Toft's post on Vine

22................Elizabeth Schreiber's post on Vine

23................................WTFVON's post on Vine

24................................Unknown Origin

25................LikeIDKWhatever's video on YouTube

26................................Chrish's post on Vine

27................................LisaMolly's post on Vine

28................Guy Jenkins' video on YouTube

29................................Nick Colleti's post on Vine

30................ChloeLMAO's post on Vine

31................Brandon Rogers' video on YouTube

32................Anthony Padilla's post on Vine

33................blackboul20's post on Vine

34................................SexyLexy's post on Vine

35................Jared Friedman's post on Vine

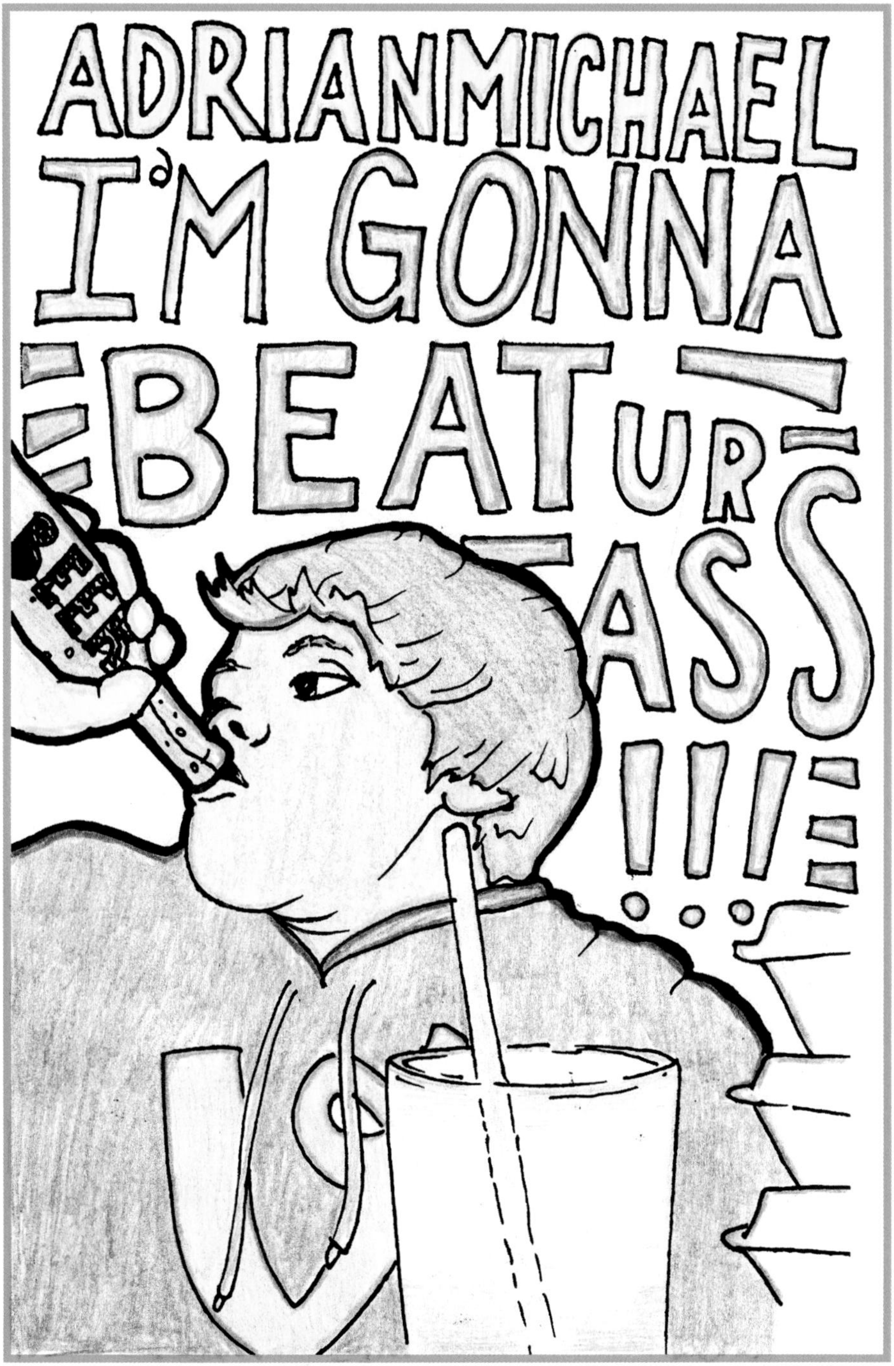
ADRIANMICHAEL
I'M GONNA
BEAT UR ASS!!!

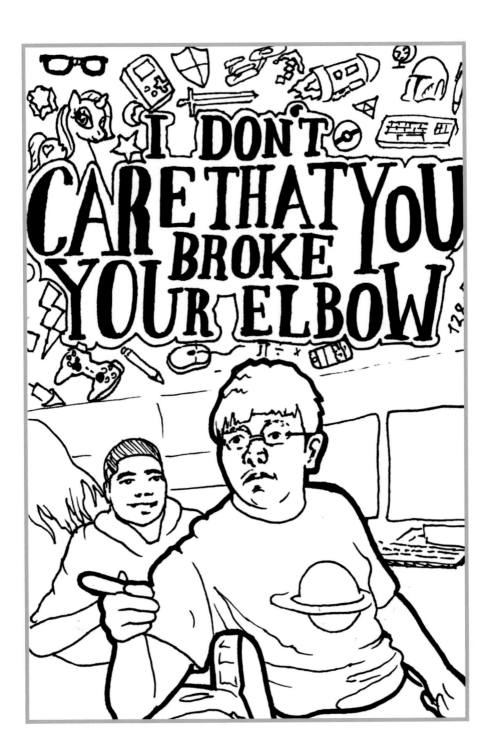

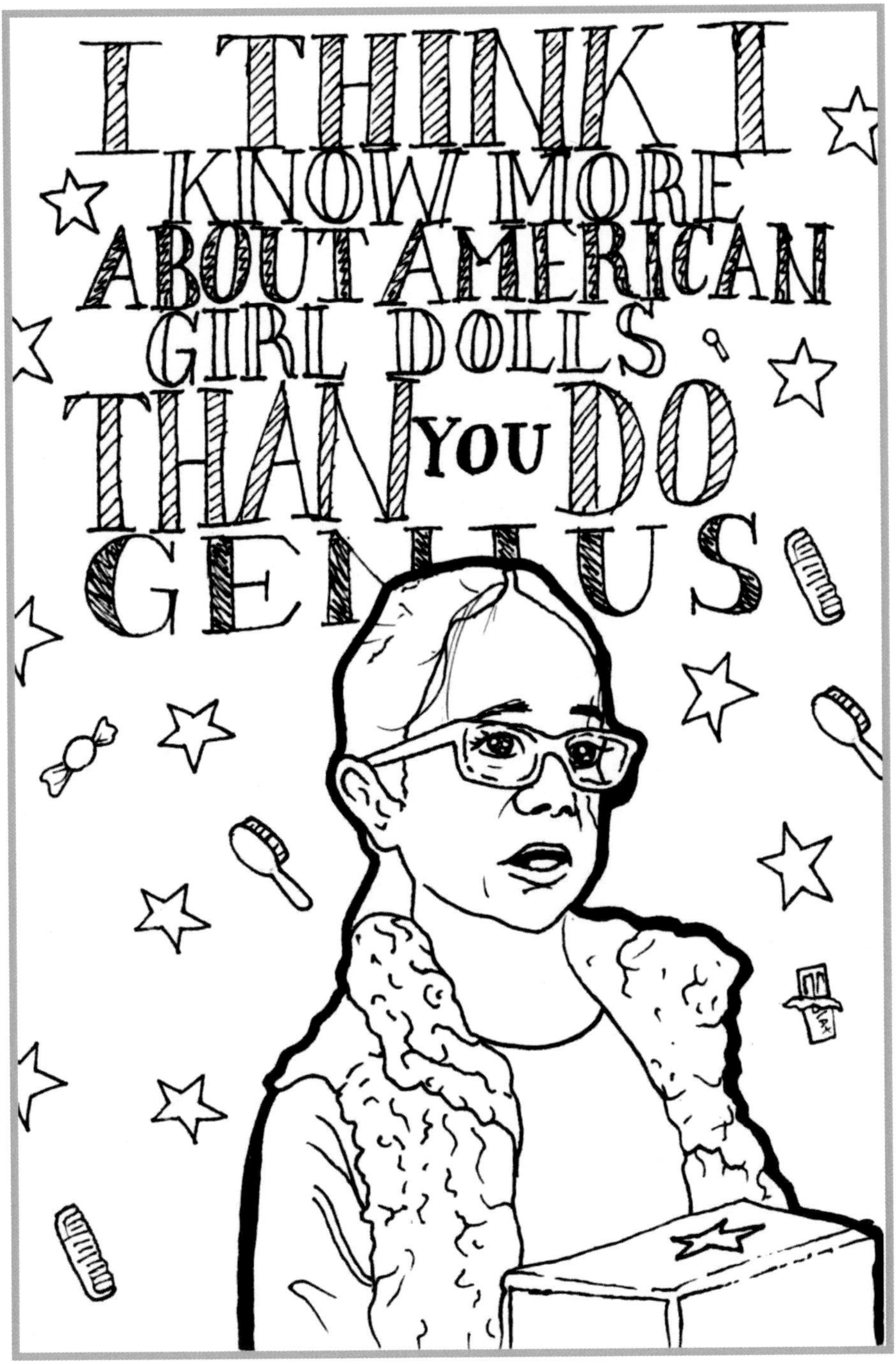
I THINK I
KNOW MORE
ABOUT AMERICAN
GIRL DOLLS
THAN YOU DO